Best Inventions

Camera

by Julie Murray

3

Dash!
LEVELED READERS
An Imprint of Abdo Zoom • abdobooks.com

Dash!
LEVELED READERS

Level 1 – Beginning
Short and simple sentences with familiar words or patterns for children who are beginning to understand how letters and sounds go together.

Level 2 – Emerging
Longer words and sentences with more complex language patterns for readers who are practicing common words and letter sounds.

Level 3 – Transitional
More developed language and vocabulary for readers who are becoming more independent.

THIS BOOK CONTAINS
RECYCLED MATERIALS

abdobooks.com

Published by Abdo Zoom, a division of ABDO, PO Box 398166, Minneapolis, Minnesota 55439.
Copyright © 2023 by Abdo Consulting Group, Inc. International copyrights reserved in all countries.
No part of this book may be reproduced in any form without written permission from the publisher.
Dash!™ is a trademark and logo of Abdo Zoom.

Printed in the United States of America, North Mankato, Minnesota.
102022
012023

Photo Credits: Alamy, Getty Images, Shutterstock
Production Contributors: Kenny Abdo, Jennie Forsberg, Grace Hansen, John Hansen
Design Contributors: Candice Keimig, Neil Klinepier, Colleen McLaren

Library of Congress Control Number: 2022937316

Publisher's Cataloging in Publication Data

Names: Murray, Julie, author.
Title: Camera / by Julie Murray
Description: Minneapolis, Minnesota : Abdo Zoom, 2023 | Series: Best inventions | Includes online resources and index.
Identifiers: ISBN 9781098280178 (lib. bdg.) | ISBN 9781098280703 (ebook) | ISBN 9781098281007 (Read-to-Me ebook)
Subjects: LCSH: Cameras--History--Juvenile literature. | Inventions--Juvenile literature. | Images, Photographic--Juvenile literature. | Inventions--History--Juvenile literature.
Classification: DDC 770.9--dc23

Table of Contents

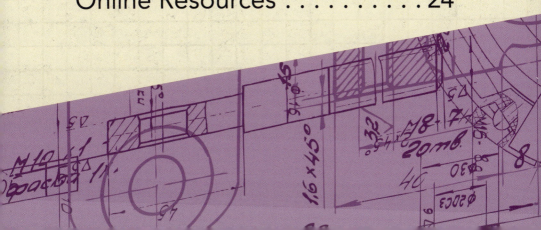

Camera

From American **Civil War** battles to everyday moments, the camera has recorded pieces of history since its invention.

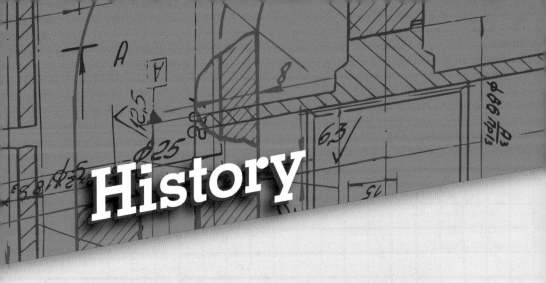

History

Joseph Nicéphore Niépce was a French inventor. He made the first camera in 1816. Niépce used metal plates to capture images. The process he used is called **heliography**.

In 1885, George Eastman invented the film camera. He called it the Kodak. Eastman's film stored images that could then be turned into **negatives**.

Steven Sasson invented the digital camera in 1975. The camera was big and weighed more than eight pounds (3.6 kg)! Its images were stored on a **cassette** tape.

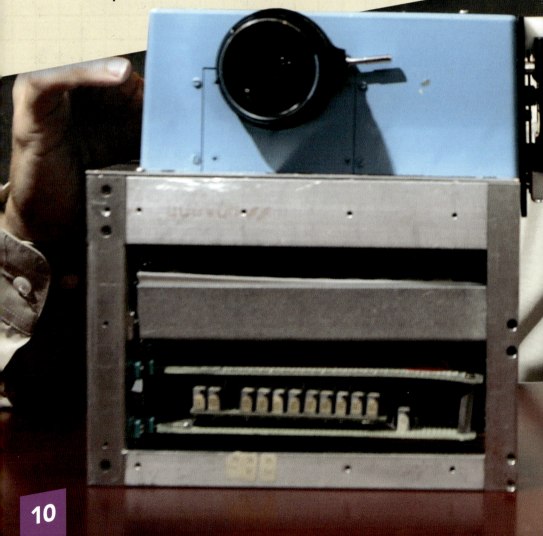

11

Today, most people take pictures with the camera on their phone. These digital photos can be printed or stored on a computer. They can also be shared with others instantly.

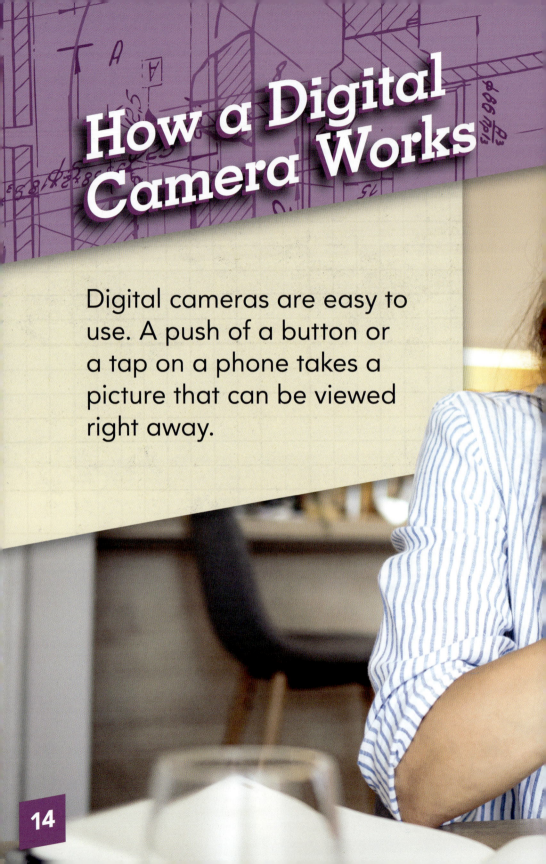

How a Digital Camera Works

Digital cameras are easy to use. A push of a button or a tap on a phone takes a picture that can be viewed right away.

15

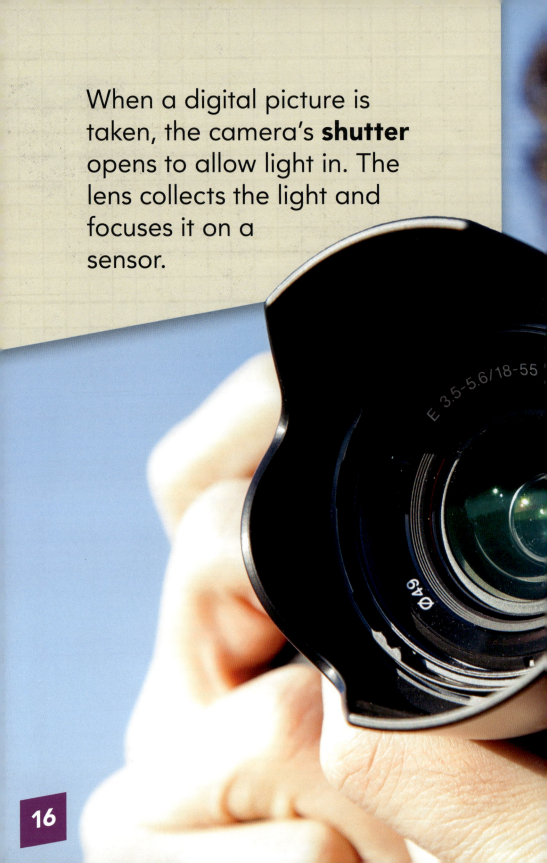

When a digital picture is taken, the camera's **shutter** opens to allow light in. The lens collects the light and focuses it on a sensor.

E 3.5-5.6/18-55

Ø 49

3200px x 2400px

1500px x 1000px

The sensor absorbs the light and the image is captured. It does this by converting the light into millions of **pixels**. The more pixels an image has, the sharper and more detailed it is.

The invention of the camera has allowed people to record events as they happen. The images captured have brought history to life and shaped our memories.

21

- The oldest surviving picture was taken in 1826. Niépce's *View from the Window at Le Gras* was taken in France.

- An instant camera uses special self-developing film. It develops a print shortly after the picture is taken. You can watch as the picture appears!

- The word camera comes from *camera obscura*, which is Latin for "dark chamber."

Glossary

cassette – a case with film, audio tape, or video tape inside.

civil war – a war between groups in the same country. The United States of America and the Confederate States of America fought a civil war from 1861–1865.

heliography – an early photographic process producing a photoengraving on a metal plate coated with an asphalt preparation.

negative – a photographic image on which light areas of the original subject appear dark and dark areas appear light. Negatives are used to make prints.

pixel – one of the tiny dots of light that make up an image on a screen. A pixel is the smallest unit of an image.

shutter – a device that opens and closes the lens of a camera. The shutter opens to let light onto the film or a sensor.

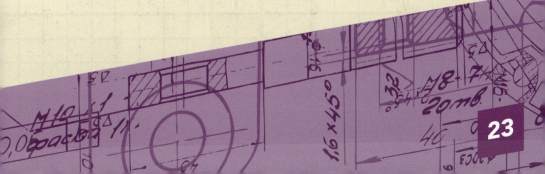

Index

Online Resources

To learn more about cameras, please visit **abdobooklinks.com** or scan this QR code. These links are routinely monitored and updated to provide the most current information available.